Common Sense

Government

For The

Common Man

Ideas For Working Class America

(Or)

You better read this before you vote!

Written By:

Greg Mims

Written by Greg Mims

ISBN 978-1-4357-1363-5

Contents

Introduction

The purpose of this book is to point out to the common, working class Americans-the backbone of this great country- the problems in our current government, which are evident and obvious, but also to encourage these millions of people that there are solutions to our problems and we can change what is wrong with our system. It only takes common sense voters to elect common sense leaders. This book will not be a deep essay that will confuse the average person. We have too much legalese these days. This book also will not be a book of lists of government abuse. If you keep up with government enough to purchase this book, then you have the working knowledge you need to understand what I am saying and you do not need me or anyone else to list every individual instance of abuse.

This book is simple. Government should be simple. We elect leaders. Leaders vote the will of their constituency. Period! They represent-that's all. There will be many who will say that these ideas presented here are great in theory but will never work in reality, because our system is just to complicated and complex for simple ideas. These are the same people who will continue to benefit themselves as long as they can keep the American people confused and disinterested.

You see, I am not the most intelligent person on the earth, nor do I claim to be. It seems to me, though, that some old fashioned common sense introduced into our current leadership might begin a change that would make right some of the wrongs that have become apparent.

You do not have to look very hard to find corruption and quagmire in our "politics as usual" system. Pork barrel spending created by logrolling has escalated to proportions that are absolutely ridiculous and has resulted in million dollar catfish farms in Arizona and the infamous bridge to nowhere in Alaska that has now been scrapped, yet the state keeps the money to use for anything it wants. Our spending has gone out of control. Is this so surprising, though, when our elected leaders vote themselves pay raises with no accountability?

Why not, when our elected leaders receive the same paycheck for a pension after they leave office, and keep receiving it until they die? How about the bribery scandals? For every one that gets caught and makes the news, there are probably another ten that do no get caught and you and I never hear about them. What about the sex scandals? They are rampant and we are hearing about more all the time. Every career politician is in it for themselves and not because they want to serve their country or you the people. You see, the problem with our government is greed and dishonesty.

Our current President is in the pocket of big business, as are most of the senators and representatives. If they aren't yet, then they are working to put themselves in that position. Hey, it's very lucrative.

Lobbyists spend millions(some in bribes) to get votes cast their way. Can you imagine what Exxon/Mobil spends in lobby each year to protect their business and keep gasoline prices inflated to $3 a gallon. They made $39.5 BILLION in PROFIT in 2006. That's **BILLION** with a **B** in **PROFIT**.

Let me help you wrap your mind around that number. 1 billion is equal to 1000 millions!!! Basically, if you can imagine 1 million dollars forty thousand times over, you have their profit.

They are number 1 on Forbes list of businesses in revenues with $370 Billion. Hey, wait a minute before you go preaching the virtues of a capitalistic society. I am right there with you, however, price fixing and gouging by all the oil companies keeps the prices and the profits high while **you and I** pay the price for their insatiable greed. This also hurts our economy tremendously because the average, working American can't afford to put money back into the economy when we are putting all of our money into our gas tank. (Keep in mind that the profit figures come after all expenses have been taken out including research and development into alternative fuel sources.)

This is just one small example of one topic that I will touch on in this book. The underlying problem behind the issues discussed here in this book is people. People think differently, have differing opinions and viewpoints and experiences, but most of us want the same thing. We want a safe country to live in where we can work and get ahead and raise our kids and be happy. Career politicians would have you believe that is what they want for us also, but the truth is that they do not care about you or I as long as they can continue to stuff their wallets with our money.

How many times have you heard in the last twenty years that a politician is running because the American people want change? Of all those that we elected, how much change did they bring about? NADA. Zilch. Zero. No change at all in any category. The funny thing is that I heard a republican in the race for the nomination the other day talking about how the American people want change in their government, yet the republicans are in the White House. I have usually voted republican although I do not consider myself affiliated with either party. It was shameful to me to hear this candidate talking about change, when everyone knows he just wants to get the money and power for himself. He will not change his party nor will he change the country.

Hillary will not bring change! Obama will not bring change! John will not bring change! They do not want change. They want to win the election and that is all. Then they will go back to doing what it is that they do the rest of the time when they are not out lying(campaigning)-powermongering.

The only time you will see change for the better in the political system in this great country is when we have an opportunity to change the system itself. Then we could start voting for the right candidate instead of trying to choose the lesser of the evils.

Most of us are not rich and some probably never will be, but the majority of us in the middle class are comfortable and trying to be happy. As long as we are not complacent, that is great, but when we become so comfortable that we become uninvolved, then we give up our opportunity to make changes for the better. You can make a difference. Your vote does count **if you vote**. Together, we as a group, the working class, are the largest group in this country, and if we work as a unit, we can affect positive change in our leadership and the direction of our great nation. Get involved now before it is to late.

The underlying purpose of this book is to cause you to honestly assess our system, question it, and foster public debate. As any good book on politics should, I hope to encourage Americans to think and act-not just on what is written here within these pages, but what is in your heart and soul-your conscience. Regardless of whether you agree with me or not, you have a place and a say in our government, and you deserve to be heard.

I encourage you to read this book and then think. Think hard about what you can do in service to your community. Think hard about your own honesty instead of trying to get ahead by abusing the system(individual ethics). The set of values that our country was founded on will bring us back in line with a government by the people and for the people. It all just comes down to common sense.

<u>God bless America!!!</u>

**The Declaration of Independence of the Thirteen Colonies
In CONGRESS, July 4, 1776**

The unanimous Declaration of the thirteen united States of America,

When in the Course of human events, it becomes necessary for one people to dissolve the political bands which have connected them with another, and to assume among the powers of the earth, the separate and equal station to which the Laws of Nature and of Nature's God entitle them, a decent respect to the opinions of mankind requires that they should declare the causes which impel them to the separation.

We hold these truths to be self-evident, that all men are created equal, that they are endowed by their Creator with certain unalienable Rights, that among these are Life, Liberty and the pursuit of

Happiness. --That to secure these rights, Governments are instituted among Men, deriving their just powers from the consent of the governed, --That whenever any Form of Government becomes destructive of these ends, it is the Right of the People to alter or to abolish it, and to institute new Government, laying its foundation on such principles and organizing its powers in such form, as to them shall seem most likely to effect their Safety and Happiness. Prudence, indeed, will dictate that Governments long established should not be changed for light and transient causes; and accordingly all experience hath shewn, that mankind are more disposed to suffer, while evils are sufferable, than to right themselves by abolishing the forms to which they are accustomed. But when a long train of abuses and usurpations, pursuing invariably the same Object evinces a design to reduce them under absolute Despotism, it is their right, it is their duty, to throw off such Government, and to provide new Guards for their future security. —Such has been the patient sufferance of these Colonies; and such is now the necessity which constrains them to alter their former Systems of Government. The history of the present King of Great Britain [George III] is a history of repeated injuries and usurpations, all having in direct object the establishment of an absolute Tyranny over these States. To prove this, let Facts be submitted to a candid world.

He has refused his Assent to Laws, the most wholesome and necessary for the public good.

He has forbidden his Governors to pass Laws of immediate and pressing importance, unless suspended in their operation till his Assent should be obtained; and when so suspended, he

has utterly neglected to attend
to them.

He has refused to pass other
Laws for the accommodation
of large districts of people,
unless those people would
relinquish the right of
Representation in the
Legislature, a right
inestimable to them and
formidable to tyrants only.

He has called together
legislative bodies at places
unusual, uncomfortable, and
distant from the depository of
their public Records, for the
sole purpose of fatiguing them
into compliance with his
measures.

He has dissolved
Representative Houses
repeatedly, for opposing with
manly firmness his invasions
on the rights of the people.

He has refused for a long time,
after such dissolutions, to
cause others to be elected;
whereby the Legislative
powers, incapable of
Annihilation, have returned to

the People at large for their exercise; the State remaining in the mean time exposed to all the dangers of invasion from without, and convulsions within.

He has endeavoured to prevent the population of these States; for that purpose obstructing the Laws for Naturalization of Foreigners; refusing to pass others to encourage their migrations hither, and raising the conditions of new Appropriations of Lands.

He has obstructed the Administration of Justice, by refusing his Assent to Laws for establishing Judiciary powers.

He has made Judges dependent on his Will alone, for the tenure of their offices, and the amount and payment of their salaries.

He has erected a multitude of New Offices, and sent hither swarms of Officers to harass our people, and eat out their substance.

He has kept among us, in times of peace, Standing Armies without the consent of our legislatures.

He has affected to render the Military independent of and superior to the Civil power.

He has combined with others to subject us to a jurisdiction foreign to our constitution and unacknowledged by our laws; giving his Assent to their Acts of pretended Legislation:

For Quartering large bodies of armed troops among us:

For protecting them, by a mock Trial, from punishment for any Murders which they should commit on the Inhabitants of these States:

For cutting off our Trade with all parts of the world:

For imposing Taxes on us without our Consent:

For depriving us, in many cases, of the benefits of Trial by Jury:

For transporting us beyond Seas to be tried for pretended offences:

For abolishing the free System of English Laws in a neighbouring Province, establishing therein an Arbitrary government, and enlarging its Boundaries so as to render it at once an example and fit instrument for introducing the same absolute rule into these Colonies:

For taking away our Charters, abolishing our most valuable Laws, and altering fundamentally the Forms of our Governments:

For suspending our own Legislatures, and declaring themselves invested with power to legislate for us in all cases whatsoever.

He has abdicated Government here, by declaring us out of his Protection and waging War against us.

He has plundered our seas, ravaged our Coasts, burnt our

towns, and destroyed the lives of our people.

He is at this time transporting large Armies of foreign Mercenaries to compleat the works of death, desolation and tyranny, already begun with circumstances of Cruelty and perfidy scarcely paralleled in the most barbarous ages, and totally unworthy the Head of a civilized nation.

He has constrained our fellow Citizens taken Captive on the high Seas to bear Arms against their Country, to become the executioners of their friends and Brethren, or to fall themselves by their Hands.

He has excited domestic insurrections amongst us, and has endeavoured to bring on the inhabitants of our frontiers, the merciless Indian Savages, whose known rule of warfare, is an undistinguished destruction of all ages, sexes and conditions.

In every stage of these Oppressions We have Petitioned for Redress in the most humble terms: Our repeated Petitions have been answered only by repeated injury. A Prince whose character is thus marked by every act which may define a Tyrant, is unfit to be the ruler of a free people.

Nor have We been wanting in attentions to our British brethren. We have warned them from time to time of attempts by their legislature to extend an unwarrantable jurisdiction over us. We have reminded them of the circumstances of our emigration and settlement here. We have appealed to their native justice and magnanimity, and we have conjured them by the ties of our common kindred to disavow these usurpations, which, would inevitably interrupt our connections and correspondence. They too have been deaf to the voice of justice and of consanguinity.

We must, therefore, acquiesce in the necessity, which denounces our Separation, and hold them, as we hold the rest of mankind, Enemies in War, in Peace Friends.

We, therefore, the Representatives of the united States of America, in General Congress, Assembled, appealing to the Supreme Judge of the world for the rectitude of our intentions, do, in the Name, and by the Authority of the good People of these Colonies, solemnly publish and declare, That these United Colonies are, and of Right ought to be Free and Independent States; that they are Absolved from all Allegiance to the British Crown, and that all political connection between them and the State of Great Britain, is and ought to be totally dissolved; and that as Free and Independent States, they have full Power to levy War, conclude Peace, contract Alliances, establish Commerce, and to do all other Acts and

Things which Independent States may of right do. And for the support of this Declaration, with a firm reliance on the protection of divine Providence, we mutually pledge to each other our Lives, our Fortunes and our sacred Honor.

The signers of the Declaration represented the new states as follows:

New Hampshire

Josiah Bartlett, William Whipple, Matthew Thornton

Massachusetts

John Hancock, Samuel Adams, John Adams, Robert Treat Paine, Elbridge Gerry

Rhode Island

Stephen Hopkins, William Ellery

Connecticut

**Roger Sherman, Samuel
Huntington, William Williams,
Oliver Wolcott**

New York

**William Floyd, Philip
Livingston, Francis Lewis,
Lewis Morris**

New Jersey

**Richard Stockton, John
Witherspoon, Francis
Hopkinson, John Hart,
Abraham Clark**

Pennsylvania

**Robert Morris, Benjamin Rush,
Benjamin Franklin, John
Morton, George Clymer, James
Smith, George Taylor, James
Wilson, George Ross**

Delaware

**Caesar Rodney, George Read,
Thomas McKean**

Maryland

Samuel Chase, William Paca, Thomas Stone, Charles Carroll of Carrollton

Virginia

George Wythe, Richard Henry Lee, Thomas Jefferson, Benjamin Harrison, Thomas Nelson, Jr., Francis Lightfoot Lee, Carter Braxton

North Carolina

William Hooper, Joseph Hewes, John Penn

South Carolina

Edward Rutledge, Thomas Heyward, Jr., Thomas Lynch, Jr., Arthur Middleton

Georgia

Button Gwinnett, Lyman Hall, George Walton

The Two Party System

The two party system is nothing new. It has been around for millennia and various forms of it have been utilized in many governments over the last four to five thousand years. Of course, back then, instead of beating your adversary in an election, you just assassinated him or her and assumed power. We have evolved somewhat in the past thousand years. Now we don't actually kill our political enemies physically-we just hang out their dirty laundry for CNN or Fox news to pick up and the political career is as good as over-or is it?

In our own history, the two parties started out as the Whigs and the Tories. This type of system was supposed to serve as a "checks and balance" for our government. Through the years, the names have changed and certain ideas with them, but the basics of the two party system remain intact to this day, right, wrong, or indifferent.

The system itself is a good one that served its purpose during the early stages of our history, but now needs to be altered somewhat. There are some shortcomings that I have noticed and changes that need to be made. One of these shortcomings is that our elected leaders have discovered that they can keep all the power for themselves as long as they agree to work together to do so. This power was originally supposed to be in the hands of the people. If you study our founding fathers, you will find that they warned about the possible abuse of this power that would inevitably arise from this system-the very abuse that we witness today. Our elected leaders may play partisan politics and blame each other for everything, but when it comes to the actual operation of government, they vote together to keep it the same. (This is the same thing as price fixing by major players of an industry.) Of course, the biggest power that congress maintains is control over tax dollars.

Another shortcoming I see is that we do not have representatives of all the people. Through the evolution of the parties, there have come to be many subgroups within each party. These subgroups have attempted to segregate the parties and divide them into fractional sub parties. In other words, the far right and the far left have attempted to take their respective party to the corners away from the middle ground and the general ideas and values that the majority of party members believe in. The moderates in each party have attempted to keep the parties together with middle of the road values and ideas. Occasionally, one of the extreme groups will pull away from the party and support another candidate that represents their agenda more specifically.

Let me give you an example to help you understand. Since I have usually voted Republican (I am not a member of the Republican party and have voted for Democrats several times along the way), let me use them as the example. Right wing Republicans, otherwise known as extreme conservatives, have attempted in the past to push for right wing conservatives to head their party and run for office. It is happening right now with the far right pushing hard for Mike Huckabee in the primaries. This is great and they should attempt to have a candidate that shares their values. I personally feel that we would be much better off if our country were more conservative. However, when the far right decides to vote for a candidate that has little chance of winning in the general election, they splinter the group. The same thing happens on the left.

This is what our two party system has become. Our founding fathers wanted it to be a proper system that would offer choices, and compromise would be the great result. We are now getting results that we can't live with.

We could establish a four party system. I am sure that someone would get smart though, and figure out how to re-unite their party to secure victory.

The best solution would be to have a three party system. This system would be made up of the left party, the right party, and the moderate party. We then could elect a President by popular vote(no electoral college), and a Vice President from each of the other two parties(these vice-presidents would have a much greater role in the political process.) This would give a more accurate "checks and balance," give us better representation, and would work much better for the national referendums which I will propose later in this book.

The most important thing we could do through this proposed system is to bring about a real, significant, and lasting change, giving the power back to the people.

None of the leaders in the past thirty-two years have brought about real change, because they have no true vision of the future of the people of America. They see only the future of the rich and powerful. It is the "god complex."

We have people like Ted Kennedy and Larry Craig-just two examples of the types of leaders we elect. Ted Kennedy has his Chappaquiddick, and Larry Craig has his bathroom stall(he still swears he is not gay). It is on both sides of the aisle, and is rampant among our elected officials, because they feel they are above the law and above any moral reproach. They have no rules because they are the rule makers! They are not accountable to their constituents at all. I will be talking about this in more detail in the next chapter.

So you see, the real underlying problem is not just with our two party system, but also with the men and women who sit high above us and make our laws and spend our money and continually tell us that they know what is best for us.

I dare say it is time for "we the people" to stand up and say that they do not represent what is best for us and we can better represent ourselves. We have to have a system that will keep the career politicians honest. We cannot trust them to police themselves. We cannot trust them to do what is in our best interests. We must give the power back to the people. Keep reading and you will understand what I mean.

The Problems With Our Government

Anyone with any common sense at all can see that all problems are a result of people. Hold on before you get on your high horse. I am not saying we need to get rid of all the people! I happen to be one and I like being here. No…I am saying that people cause problems and people have to fix those problems. I dare say that ALL of our problems in government as well as all other areas of our lives can be made better or fixed completely with just three things. These three things are:

1. complete and total honesty, (not politically correct for fear of offending someone-hey, the truth hurts sometimes)
2. responsibility, and
3. accountability.

This is common sense!

In today's world of politics, scandals are everywhere and on the news everyday. Our politicians speak out of both sides of their mouths while they stuff money in all of their pockets. It is disgraceful to "We the People" to have our leaders behaving worse than children. Even our best leaders are in it for themselves and not for the people. Here are some of the major underlying problems that we face with our current government and some of the solutions we the people can bring about.

1.   Career Politicians.

We have allowed our "public servants" to become career oriented in that profession. It has become a job with a very lucrative salary for many who get elected to higher office. These career politicians also gain power whereby they may continue to create more streams of income from their influence, as well as help out their friends by appointing them to high positions within various government organizations or ensuring lucrative government contracts. It has to be a pretty good deal for all colleges to develop political science majors and completely fill their classes every semester. I suggest that politics as a career leads to corruption.

There are to many opportunities for even an honest person to get sucked into the temptation. By the time a person has risen from the local school board to city council, they have learned how to "logroll" (you vote for me on this and I will vote for you on that) with the best of them. This is a practice that goes beyond compromise. They also have learned how to vote to keep themselves in power and still sound on the news like they are there for the people. It's a perpetual gravy train that the working class supports with our complacency. And why not, when we feel as though our vote doesn't count for anything anymore. Even if our candidate wins, we soon feel disassociated with them because they are looking out for their own future interests. They forget the people!

And they develop superman mentality. I described it earlier as the "god complex." They are invincible and above the law or any morals.

2.   Money.

Money is not the root of all evil. The love of money is though, and our career politicians love money. Whether they got involved in politics to get inside tracks to further their own businesses, or they are just living off the fat of the land(taxes), they all are profiting largely in their chess game.

There is so much money now being thrown at politicians, it would be almost impolite to turn it down, right? Lobbyists spend literally millions and possibly even billions every year to ensure that politicians vote a certain way. Of course, there have been numerous news reports about politicians that have taken bribes from lobbyists. These reports include everything from home repairs to rent for an apartment that was never actually occupied.

Money sees no political party affiliation either. The Republicans and Democrats alike are all getting their share. I am convinced there is not an honest, ethical one in the bunch. Of course all the right wing conservatives hail George W. Bush as being honest and ethical, but he is just as much in the pocket of big business as any of the others. (I believe he is a good man, and probably a Christian man, but so was Jimmy Carter, and they both turned out to be pretty bad Presidents.) I voted for him so I can say that.

If you don't believe that greed and dishonesty are the policy of the day, then explain to me the midnight vote for a pay raise for our congressman and women. Don't tell me you've forgotten about that one. I sure haven't. Explain to me why they each receive exactly the same pay for their pension as they got when they were actively serving(I use that term loosely). That sounds like a good deal to me. Why can't we get all Americans in on that deal? Because it is only for the privileged, fortunate few of the "bourgoise." This is your tax money at work! HA! Or should I say that these are your politicians working your tax money?

Rest assured, they are going to get their fair share as long as we allow it to continue. As long as politicians are allowed to make lucrative salaries and vote to keep themselves in power regardless of the people's wishes, they will continue to accept bribes, vote for big business lobbies, give tax breaks to themselves and their buddies(lobbyists), and put the burden of funding America on the backs of the working people. I'm sorry, but I can't help but be reminded of the history lessons I was taught about slavery. It all sounds familiar.

Don't go running for your gun because there is a communist or socialist afoot. I am not either. I am a capitalist, but I understand quite clearly how insatiable greed, dishonesty, and catering to special interest groups can quickly turn capitalism into payoffs to make the playing field uneven.

This country was founded on equal opportunity and the idea that all men are created equal. The civil rights movement was also established on the equal rights of all men and women. How then, can we sit back and continue to elect officials that stuff their pockets and vote to maintain a playing field that is kept unequal for the benefit of big business and the already rich who are getting richer? This current system allows them to keep the power and the money and prevents "we the people" from raising our eyebrows.

3.   Voting.

Why is it that fewer and fewer voters are turning out at the polls to vote? Why is it that fewer and fewer people of voting age are registering to vote? It is because they feel now more than ever before that their vote does not count at all. Our citizens feel like they don't make a difference, that they don't have a say in the operation of our government. And why is that? It is because all politicians lie! Maybe they have not been caught yet, but they do lie. Remember, we are being completely honest with ourselves here. They call it campaigning. They promise us "this, that, and the other thing" to paraphrase one of my favorite episodes of Gilligan's Island. That is a perfect analogy. These campaigns are just like an episode of Gilligan's Island.

Promises, Promises! They promise change! They say things like "America wants change. America needs change. America needs our candidate, 'fill in the blank,' to step in and steer this ship in a new direction. We see a new sunset on the horizon! "Fill in the blank" will lead us to a new tomorrow!"

The only tomorrow that any of these idiot candidates are leading us to is a bankrupt continuation of the same old business as usual politics.

Think with me honestly again for a moment. How many campaigns have you lived through in your lifetime so far? Personally, I have lived through ten Presidential elections in my lifetime. I have voted in six. I remember the campaigns as far back as the 1976 election in which Jimmy Carter won the Presidency. He ran on a campaign of change and peace. That was really important then considering the Vietnam War, Nixon's near impeachment, and all.

I would say it is somewhat important now also, considering the Iraq war, the war on terror, Afghanistan, Turkey, Iran, North Korea, Pakistan, India, Israel, Palestine, Jordan, Syria, and probably about a dozen other hotbeds that I forgot to mention. People now want change just like they did then. Did we get it? No, but we did get super long lines at the gas pumps with terribly inflated prices.

What about 1980? Ronald Reagan promised to bring about change and an end to the Iran hostage crisis. He did that and we actually did see change in our economy for the good also. We entered one of the most prosperous times in our nations history. Reagan beefed up our military and operated from a position of strength in most cases. A lot of people had jobs then that don't now! We started advancing technologically and people were learning to adapt to the new and coming global economy. We were pretty prosperous. He was conservative and the far right discovered their champion. In all, we were prosperous and it was good. But was that really Reagan's doing? The truth is that the economic boom came when the technology began to increase at a tremendous rate and new and innovative products began flooding the markets making our lives "easier."

What about 1988? All George H. Bush had to do was come in on a white horse and ride out the prosperity wagon while we read his lips with "No New Taxes." What a crock! He did not run on a campaign of change. He won. It was back to politics as usual. He talked out of both sides of his mouth and he will be remembered as the President who probably has had more playings of his sound bite than any other President. Maybe "we the people" just didn't know how to read lips. Mr. Bush started sending jobs overseas.

Of course, he was not the only one. 1992 saw Bill Clinton ride on the change campaign. By then, America wanted and needed change. We got some change and some more of the same. We were still pretty prosperous overall but the military was being closed down base by base and civilian jobs cut drastically. Other jobs were still being sent overseas, but our president could play the saxophone and really liked Fleetwood Mac. He also really liked a certain intern. He did not like, however, Vince Foster. The Republicans smelled blood and used his lack of morals to squeek out the election in 2000 under a campaign of "change."

Enter the current administration of George W. Bush. The big businessman himself and all his big business friends have had a heyday at the expense of the working middle class. It's ok though, because while the middle class was growing at a much lesser rate, his friends were getting much richer by the day. Can you say Exxon-Mobil? He is only as "Green" as his next dollar. He also is in love with the immigrants from south of the border.

So what do we have to look forward to in our candidates for the 2008 Presidential election? Business as usual with no change-that's Democrats, Republicans, and anyone else who may try a libertarian ticket. Why? Because every one of them intends to keep the power to themselves and the governing bodies of the Senate and the House of Representatives instead of giving it back to the people where it belongs.

Hillary Clinton will not bring change. Barack Obama will not bring change. John Mccain will not bring change. Change is not in their own personal best interests. None of these will be willing to change our government to give the power back to the people to decide our nation's policies.

The democrats will try to give millions of illegal immigrants amnesty and talk about national health care but not come up with a way to pay for it without taxing America to the hilt. The republicans will promise tax cuts that only the rich will actually receive. Some of them will ride the marriage issue. Some will ride the second amendment gun issue which is nothing new for the GOP. Each side will blame the other for not being able to get anything accomplished. In reality, there will be no change.

As I write this, I remember that today is Veterans' Day, a day that we honor those who have served in our country's armed forces. What did they serve for? They served so that "we the people" would be free to exercise our rights and live without fear of oppression and tyranny, yet we surrender ourselves to the tyranny of a system that does not allow the people to decide on the major issues. Our politicians speak for us. I'm sorry, but we seem to now be speaking a different language. The people must come back to vote and overwhelmingly vote out all career politicians.

The political office is a privilege and responsibility to anyone who dares to take it. It is a position of trust and service to our country. A political office should be nothing more than a representation of the constituents of the area. It is **not** a job of security and power and money any more than it is a stepping stone for future aspirations. American citizens need to take back their authority they have given to the elected officials, and we need to determine for ourselves the courses we should take.

We have to be totally and completely honest with ourselves and others(not politically correct), take the responsibility for our government and it's leaders by voting and getting involved, and hold them accountable for their actions and their voting.

We too have to be accountable for our actions as citizens. Our individual ethics must be above board to effect change in our societies. We have to get away from the "what's in it for me" mentality, and move into a "what's is best for our society" type of thinking. Only then can we truly foster peace within our nation, and work together for a promising future.

Solutions To Our Problems

Now that we have discussed a few of the very basic problems with our government in a common sense way, we need to come up with some real, practical, common sense solutions to these problems. I will be the first to tell you that I don't have all the answers. I will also tell you that anyone who says he or she does have all the answers is just another lying(campaigning) career politician. Let's think about solutions for the common working class person or family, because we represent the majority of America and we pay most of the taxes. Keep that in mind as you read- **WE ARE THE MAJORITY!!! We can effect change!**

To address the problem of individuals making a career out of politics instead of serving their country, we must address the lure to be a politician. What does lure one to become a career politician? **Power and money.** OK!

Let's start with power because as long as one has too much power, he or she can use that power to influence money. How do we curtail the power of our politicians and give it back to the people? The number one way to curb the power wielding of our elected officials is to set term limits on every elected office regardless of how high or low the station. My proposal is to set term limits for the nationally elected officials and state elected officials that cannot be changed by those officials. In other words, a law restricting term limits that can only be changed by a majority vote in a national referendum. I think we should extend the term of the President to five years with a maximum of two terms that he or she can serve. Unlike the current situation, a President would not be eligible to run again after the second term even in time of war, simply because we have seen how a President can orchestrate a war if they so desire. Two terms-ten years-you're gone!

I also propose the same for the Senate and House of Representatives. Each election would be held during the third year-middle year of the presidential term. The term of both Senators and Representatives would be five years, and each would be eligible to be elected to two terms max. Two terms-ten years-you're gone! Out with the old and in with the new. Strom Thurmond and Ted Kennedy would never make it with me around.

The same laws would apply to the state governors as does the President, and to the state Senate and House as it did to the Federal houses, except the voting would be statewide.

All other elected posts would be obligated to follow suit and set two term limits for an individual. No career posts!

There is another way to curtail the power of federal government. As I stated earlier, there would be three parties. These would be the left, the right, and the moderate parties. Instead of two houses of congress, there would be three-one for each party. Each of these houses would have 100 members. That's a total of 300 congressmen and women instead of the 535 we have now. (That alone would save a few dollars in payroll and pensions.) Each of these party houses would come together and debate each issue and then come up with their best plan for each major issue. These three plans would then be aired out on the national newscasts, and then be put to the people for a vote in a national referendum. The people would have a choice of the three plans and would have the final say. Obviously, we can't take off work ten times a year to go vote so the major issues would be voted on in one day each year called national referendum day. We will get to some examples of the major issues in more detail later, but right now let's take just one example.

Abortion seems to be a great example because it doesn't involve economics or national security, but rather the moral consciousness of America and it's citizenry. Also, because this issue is such a hotly debated one in virtually all states, a national viewpoint should be taken to settle the issue. The job of your elected officials then changes from voting what they think, or what they "logrolled" for, to putting together a bill for the national referendum so "we the people" can decide what "we the people" want in this particular scenario. Our Supreme Court would not have the say in these matters.

(I just thought of a good logrolling example to help you out. Senator A from Massachusetts goes to Senator B from Utah and tells him or her, "hey, I will vote for your anti-abortion bill if you will vote for my gay marriage bill. The Senator from Utah replies, "O.k., I will vote for your gay marriage bill, but only if you include a section that makes it legal also for me to have up to eighteen wives." The deal is struck.)

Sorry, I digress. Your elected official then works together with his or her other electees to come up with the best plans for the people to vote on. Notice I said plans-plural. There has to be more than one plan to vote for or the elected officials can put in something that they know no one will go for and then they have the power back. Keep in mind- **it's a game of power play to them**. We cannot give them the opportunity to give into temptation. So the three houses come up with a few options for the American people to vote on during the annual National Referendum day.

The first option is no abortion after the first trimester of pregnancy. This should take care of all cases of rape and incest as they are usually discovered during this time period and can be handled as deemed necessary by the mother or her parents if she is under the age of, I don't know, say- 14.

The second option available on the referendum would be no abortion at all except in cases of rape or incest. There may be a slight increase in the number of reported rapes and incest cases.

The third option would be abortions on demand, available at all times under any circumstances.

The point is that you get to vote instead of having the Supreme Court decide for you. I would much rather have

100 million people make that decision together than to rely on the decision of twelve justices. Wouldn't you?

Now that your legislators have done their job and gotten the possible options on the referendum, they can go play golf or chase an intern around, and leave the voting to the capable hands of the American citizens.

You now have a direct say in government and policy! The will of the people reigns supreme. A Democratic society.

Now that the vote has been taken, the bill that passed by majority vote will become effective January 1 of the next year and will remain in effect until it can come back to ballot five years later.

I joke a little, but I personally believe that this is the way that most of our pressing issues in this country should be solved. And think about it-if the vote does not go the way that you wanted it to, you will have a chance to change it five years from now when it comes up to ballot again-if there is enough support for it to come to a vote.

Once again, this is where your elected officials have to stop drinking bloody mary's and get back to work. The agenda for each years referendum is to be decided by popular opinion, and only ten(or twenty) items each year can be put on the ballot. You must take action and write or call or email your representatives and get them to put your issue at the forefront of debate to be included on the ballot.

Of course, since only ten(or twenty) items can be included on the ballot each year and the decision stands for five years before it can be voted on again, that means that next year ten(or twenty) new items can be on the agenda. If your item did not make the agenda this year, start working for next year.

The truth of this scenario is that it gets the people back involved in politics and the running of this country, and takes a large amount of power abuse out of the hands of the government. This is government **"for the people, by the people"** and it makes your vote count. Every voter counts in government "for the people by the people." This also lets our politicians know that they do not know what is best for us like they would have us believe. **They cannot and will not speak for us when we can speak for ourselves**.

The President's and the two Vice-President's roles in all of this is actually simple in design yet difficult to effect. They will be responsible for taking the pulse of the American public and making a final decision on the top five issues to be put to the ballot. That means they have to take all of the issues in question, go out among the people, and find out which ones are the most pressing and important to the people. Normally, these will be issues of national defense and security, as well as economic issues. Again, there will have to be choices of plans for the people to consider. These plans will be made available to the American public through the media prior to referendum day so the people can study and become educated on the issues. This actually should take place as the options for each plan are being considered, so the people can call in with their ideas and suggestions for the plans. States will do the same things on smaller issues that do not have national concerns and will hold statewide and local elections.

There is one other thing that will remove the abuse of power from those who govern. No appointees except to cabinet positions. No appointed judges period. All judicial positions including the Supreme Court would be elected by the people. Each party house would get to nominate three candidates. The people would decide. There would be term limits here too, and I would suggest terms of five years with a maximum of four terms. The Attorney General would be elected. No more politicizing these positions, please! And thank you very much! Find the best man or woman for the job and get the politics out of it.

The courts of the land would also not be able or have the authority to overturn any decisions made and passed in the national referendum. The courts are there to uphold the law only. They are not free to interpret the law as they see fit, nor are they free to change the law to meet demands of special interest groups or their own whims. The law is what it is and they are to rule in accordance with those laws as the people have empowered them to do. Their power is derived from the people also, and they are also accountable to the people, therefore no issue put in place by referendum shall be overturned, except by the people.

Yet another item that will give the power back to the people is the line item veto, or a form of it. In other words,

I would propose that no items that are not directly affiliated with or related to the main item of an agenda can be included in that bill.

An example for your understanding: Senator A from Georgia with a heavy southern drawl goes to Senator B from California and tells him or her, "Ahhhh seeeee you have introduced a biiiill on tax reform that is scheduled to appeeeear on the national referenduuum. Ahhhh would like to add a very smaaall fine print section to your biiiill that would give me $500 million dollaaaars for a forest preserve next to my house so Ahhhh can take you and aaaall our big buuuusiness friends hunting next yeeear. If you will do this for meee, Ahhhh will aaadd some very fine print on guuun controool and abolition of the NRAAAAAA in my biiiill on abooortion. (I am from Georgia so I can make fun of the way we talk!)

I also am an American so I can make fun of the idiot congressmen and women we elect who hide all kinds of crap in the back of bills that have nothing to do with the main topic of the bill. Look it up for yourself. It is in every bill that gets sent for ratification. How about bills that have to do with housing or something important for the people, but somewhere in the back of the bill, there is $1 million for a catfish farm or $400 million for a bridge to nowhere in Alaska. Our politicians are good at this. They get a bill and publicize it heavily in the media as a bill to help the poor. That is the main topic of the bill. What they are not telling you is that there are $10 billion worth of other junk in there that has nothing to do with the poor but making them poorer. You get the point.

No Pork and no additions-Just the bill and necessary affiliated or related items.

This just goes back to prove the lack of integrity that our elected officials have. They will tell you that this is what has to be done to get anything accomplished in Washington. That is truly a sad commentary on our government.

Anyway, any and all extras will be struck from these bills completely or they will not be allowed on the ballot for the national referendum. **Power to the people-not to the politicians!**

Now that we have discussed some ways to alleviate the lure of power abuse from the role of politician, let's look at some common sense ideas about alleviating the lure of money and greed.

Term limits could actually cause problems in this area if a person gets the idea that he or she needs to get all they can while they can. There would have to be a watchdog organization set up to track finances of all politicians. This is a great idea because, as a public servant, they have to be accountable to the American public-period! No questions. Open your checkbook and all of your financial dealings to a special section of the IRS if you want to go into political office. You will be reviewed annually to ensure that you are not taking bribes(Republican Senator Ted Stevens) or using your influence to gain an unfair advantage in business. Of course, the age-old question of " who is watching the watchdog?" comes into play. We would have to develop the system so that a different review team handles each official every year, and they do not know who that review team consists of.

I do feel that lobbyists should be able to do some things for the elected officials(I am not heartless to their plight). One 3 martini lunch a month at an expense of no more than $100 per lobby group per official should be more than sufficient for them to get their points across to the politicians. The more persuasive lobbyists could probably save a bunch of money by only doing a two martini lunch.

One thing that would have to go hand in hand with this idea though is that there would have to be punishment for violating these laws. First of all, no Presidential pardons of any kind will be allowed. We are not letting that nut job let all his or her friends go free right before he or she leaves office. If they did the crime and were convicted of it, then they will do the time just like the rest of the people. There will be no commuted sentences. There will be no special privilege. Anyone convicted of taking bribes will face mandatory minimum sentences of twenty years without parole, and they will be mixed in with the general population in prison. Let's see how they survive in that atmosphere-no federal, white collar, country club prisons. I'd be willing to bet that you would not have to many politicians soliciting bribes or taking them. Also, any monies found to be obtained outside of the parameters set forth would be confiscated and put into the general fund. No, the trophy wife does not get to keep it and marry another politician. She should have married an actor instead!

Another small change would help to keep politicians from joining the ranks just to get rich. This change would involve a big change in their pay structure and pension plan.

As you may or may not know, our United States Congress has the power and authority to vote themselves a pay raise, and they do so as they deem fitting. They make far above the national average for an individual. They also have the best pension plan in the world. It goes something like this:

> They get their regular pay when they are serving actively. Then they retire or get defeated in an election. They then receive the exact same amount as a pension beginning immediately. They continue to receive this same amount until they die. Then their spouse continues to receive this same amount until he or she dies. Give me some of that-huh!

Your tax dollars at work again! The worst part about it to me is that we have soldiers going to war and dying who make paltry salaries, yet they do it for the love of country. We have policemen and women or firemen and women who risk their lives everyday for our safety, and they get very little in return. Kinda makes you want to go out and skin a fat cat, doesn't it?

My common sense proposal to fix this problem is very simple. We pass a law by referendum stating that all U.S. congressmen and women will be paid a salary each year matching the exact median income of all Americans. If the median income for an individual in America is $50,000 per year, then that is the salary for the next year for all of the congressmen and women.

If they want a pay raise, then they have to make sure that they are doing whatever it takes to help people get jobs, and raise the national average of salaries.

In other words, when they help the overall economy of our nation, then and only then do they get a pay raise for themselves. Of course, if they slack on their job to boost the economy and the average median salary figure goes south, so too does their paycheck. I would be willing to bet that we would have some public figures who would work tooth and nail to improve our economy. (The unemployed would be figured into this equation also, which would drive the national median average down. Do you think they might try to prevent jobs from going to other countries then?)

And what will we do about this pension plan? Easy! We just do the same thing. Whatever plan for social security is in place at the time will be their plan for retirement. Again, I would be willing to wager that they would take on the challenge of fixing our social security system if this became the law. Rest assured, you would have several options for change to vote on come national referendum day.

And what about their health care plan? Obviously, we would just give them the median average health care plan(preferably an HMO) and they would have to live (or die) with it. Of course, they would have to go to the doctors in the plan.

The reasons we have these problems to address in the first place is because the elected officials are not currently required to play by the same rules that the rest of Americans have to live by. I am only proposing that we level the playing field and require them to live in the same world and play by the same rules as the rest of "**we the people**."

We have to take the power back. We must insist that these areas be changed if we are ever to expect change in the type of people who are ruining our government-yes, I said "ruining." Once we change these people, then "**we the people**" will "run" the government, and I am completely satisfied that we can do a much better job than the current leaders are doing.

Democrats and Republicans and Libertarians, it matters not. We are Americans, and as such, it is our duty to serve and take care of our fellow Americans. The true power must be in the hands of the people for this nation to remain the greatest nation in the world. We are in a new millennium and we must put in place now the foundation to build our country's future on.

The Economy

Wow, what a topic of conversation. This is one of those categories that affects everyone in this country and most everyone outside of this country. There are so many different parts of our economy that to lump it into one category would not allow us to take an in depth look at it. Let's separate it, then, into as many subcomponents as we can deal with effectively here.

American Jobs
Unemployment
Foreign Trade/Import-Export
Foreign Aid
Social Security
Welfare
Health Care/Insurance Reform
Taxes
Interest Rates
Annual Budget/Deficit

I am sure there are many more areas that we could discuss concerning the American economy, but these are the main areas of concern to the average, middle class, working American, so we will stick with these and you can research sub categories on your own if you so choose.

If you're ready, then let's get started.

American Jobs

There is one statement that we must make before all else is said, because all else is dependent on our viewpoint of this statement. Are you ready? Here it comes.

"In relation to the American economy, the American job is the most sacred thing we have."

Our entire economy is driven by the American job-not the overseas job. When one job is sent to a foreign country, the employer cuts his or her cost of production for that job, gaining more profit margin for the company. That is great for the company, and big business increases their profits while they lay off hundreds or thousands here. Those hundreds or thousands then have to find employment in a shrinking market of new or available jobs. (Have you looked at the help wanted ads lately? Are there more jobs in the paper or online nowadays or fewer?)

Those hundreds or thousands usually have to live on much less, which means they put less money into our economy. They have less disposable income with which to work. Most of these people end up having to go through some type of retraining for a different field which costs our economy even more. The end result is that the rich get richer, big business with no moral conscience makes greater profit margins, while they pump money into foreign economies and drain money and the spirit of America out of ours.

Our society has become one of such greed that people no longer matter as long as a business can turn another dollar. It is great that companies make money, and that is the objective. It is not great when companies(boards and leaders)have to make so much money that they would commit economic treason against their fellow countrymen. It is sad and shameful for them to be called Americans.

The long term effects of sending jobs overseas has not been seen yet, but the trends are starting to show that it has hurt us both in the short term, and will be worse so in the long run. The American dollar is losing strength globally, the housing market is collapsing, inflation is rising so much faster than salaries, credit is being used and abused more than ever to try to keep up, and we are headed for a recession that could turn into a depression worse than our grandparents saw in 1929 before it is all over with.

The contributing factors are many more than just sending jobs overseas, but this is one of the biggest factors, and must be stopped immediately if we are going to recover to be great again.

Think about something for just one minute. Everyone loves Wal-Mart-right? When Wal-Mart was going national, they advertised how many of their products were made in America. They built their whole customer base in this country behind the advertisements of "**made in America**."

They bankrupted K-Mart and thousands of small businesses by using this strategy.

How many Americans have lost their jobs because Wal-Mart doesn't sell "made in America" anymore?

Sure, we get a little better pricing because everything in Wal-Mart comes from China, Singapore, Taiwan, Mexico, Venezuela, Honduras, Brazil, Ecuador, or Chile. But at what cost? What have we done to ourselves?

OK. So the damage has been done now and unscrupulous business leaders will continue to do it. How do we stop it and turn the tide? How do we bring jobs back to Americans? How can we put some common sense into it to make it better? It won't be easy, but *we can do it.*

It has to start at the government level. We have to enact legislation that will stop jobs from going overseas. One way we can stop production jobs from leaving our shores is to raise import duties on all products from overseas entering the country. If we raise them enough, it would become more advantageous for those companies to have the product made here. One way that we could stop service jobs from going overseas would be to penalize companies with higher taxes if they send jobs overseas. We could impose a flat rate tax per job lost that the company would have to pay annually should they choose to boost the economy of another nation and commit economic treason.

There is a downside of this action and that would be slightly higher prices on some of our goods and services, but it would be well worthwhile <u>in the long term</u> for our country and our overall economy. And guess what the best part of it is? It would be that when you pick up the phone to get service, you would find an American that speaks English at the other end of the line. What a novel concept!!!

Unemployment

If you took the time to read the previous section, you would know that the remedies set forth there would help tremendously to alleviate much of the unemployment in this country. It is a fact that the majority of the unemployed people in the country are unskilled laborers and production type personnel. Most of the jobs that go overseas are these types of jobs. Keep the jobs here-reduce unemployment. Easy! But there is more that we can do.

Re-education and retraining are the best tools we have to create an even better work force. Not only will the work force be better, but the products and services will be better also. So how do we go about re-educating and retraining the work force of unemployed people? First and foremost, it takes money and a lot of it to fund a project this large. I am going to have to steal from some other sections here to give the answers but I will purposefully keep it as brief as possible so you won't have to re-read the same material five times.

The money is already there. There is more than enough money already in the system to fund this and other projects here at home. The problem is that our governmental leaders decide that they want to spend $400 million on a bridge to nowhere in Alaska instead of using that money for something positive for the people of this country. Our congressmen and women waste more money every year on total crap that is unnecessary. It is not the federal government's job to be stupid with our tax money, although the elected officials insist that it is.

The special interests groups will be hot about this, but let 'em get hot.

<u>The truth is the truth even if it is not politically correct to say so.</u>

Take all the money given to special interests groups, and we could fund retraining for every unemployed American. Stop giving away all of our money to foreign aid, and we could educate every American. It is not our job to fund the rest of the world's governments and economies. It is our job to take care of our own first, and then and only then, look to help others outside our borders. Every American needs and deserves a job. We have the ability to give them the skills they need to have a job and be a productive member of society and not a drain on our economy. We have to do this for them and for ourselves as a country.

Foreign Trade

Import/Export

Whether you shop at Wal-Mart, Macy's, or Neiman Marcus, you are buying foreign goods and boosting the economy of another nation. You can't avoid it. There are many products that American manufacturers have abandoned making because they cannot compete with cheap labor overseas. We have shot ourselves in the foot by choosing cheap prices. We also have shot ourselves in the foot by demanding higher and higher wages for the products we make here.

Take our big three auto makers in Detroit for example. The unions are going to cause the auto makers to shut down more and more plants, because they are not willing to help the domestic brands. Prices on cars are astronomical. The big three are reporting losses in the billions, and the workers unions are demanding more and more.

What will you demand when you no longer have a job and the union isn't around to buy you a Toyota?

Let's face it. The manufacturers have not done a good job in competing with the foreign auto makers, which is why the best selling car in America is a Toyota Camry. In fact, other than my parents, I don't know of very many people who own a domestic car. The foreign companies have beaten us in fuel economy for years, and now they are beating us in alternative fuel source vehicles, which is the future.

What I am saying with all of this is that we as a country import most of the goods we use everyday. It would be very difficult to change our buying habits and more so when the prices of alternative, American brands would be higher. But we have to do something to turn the tide and import less-export more. Again, tariffs and import duties on foreign goods is the best way to reverse the tide, and to gain ground globally. It would be painful for a little while, but **we are going to pay for our past sooner or later**. Doing it this way and now will be a lot less painful than doing it later. (Our founding fathers were in favor of import duties on all kinds of products coming into this country.)

The import duties suggested would allow American manufacturers to get back into the production of various products and be competitive. This puts people back to work, and pumps more money into our economy. Over time, with fair wages and fair pricing, we would be able to buy American, and also have our products exported for consumption around the world. Of course, foreign companies that want to build plants and produce their products here would be allowed to do so, as this would create more jobs for Americans.

We also would be able to scrutinize the imported products much more carefully.

Let's look at toys made in China. How many have been recalled just here in 2007? The toys all have excessive levels of lead paint or small parts that could possibly be ingested by children. The FDA is responsible for checking these products for compliance to US safety standards, but they have no way to handle all that they are responsible for. You see, they also are responsible for monitoring all non-prescription medicines, cosmetics, and just about every other product brought into this country. They cannot do it with the manpower that they have. You and your children are at risk with the products that are currently being imported. When we reduce the number of imported products, we will be able to test a fair sample to ensure safety standards are being complied with.

Again, you as the end user will see a slight increase in cost, but you and your children will have a safer product as a result. This alone should be reason enough to push for a change in our policies.

Foreign Aid

Big Money!!!!! Huge!!!!! We give so much money away to foreign countries that it really is not even funny. No, really. It's not. We give money away to help foreign economies. We give money away to keep some governments in place. We give money away to turn over other governments. We give a lot of money away. There are some examples where we give money with a guarantee that the recipient country agrees to purchase certain specified amounts of U.S. goods. Some see this as a flaw in our policy. I see it as one of the few strengths.

There are other issues with giving away this aid. Detractors claim that it does not reach the people that need the aid, but rather goes into the leaders private accounts. Others claim that the richer nations get the most aid and the poorer countries get less. The truth of the matter is that a large part of all the money the U.S. gives goes to private consulting firms that are supposedly working to make life better for these nations. Maybe they do. Maybe they don't do enough. I only know that we have things here that need to be fixed before we fix the problems of other nations.

Some 2006 examples that <u>do not</u> include military aid:

Israel-	2 billion 520 million
Egypt-	1 billion 795 million

Columbia-	558 million
Jordan-	461 million
Pakistan-	698 million
Peru-	133 million
Indonesia-	158 million
Kenya-	213 million
Bolivia-	122 million
Ukraine-	115 million
India-	94 million
Haiti-	163 million
Russia-	52 million
Ethiopia-	145 million
West Bank(gaza)-	150 million
Liberia-	89 million
Bangladesh-	49 million
Bosnia-	51 million

I understand the reasons behind some of this. In fact, I would go so far as to agree that some of it is necessary. The majority of it, however, is not and should stay right here within our borders to help our own people. Do you realize that we could help to fund a national health care system with this money? Do you understand that with our government not wasting our money, we could subsidize more small business ventures, thereby creating more jobs? Do you realize that we could fix our social security problem? There are many social ills that we could help with all of this money.

I feel bad for people in foreign countries when I see them on tv. I know they are poor and many go hungry. I have compassion for them. I also know that we have the same thing right here in our country, and we have the ability to fix this problem.

Our responsibility starts here at home. Again, after we have resolved our domestic issues, then we can go abroad and help solve the problems in the rest of the world. After we have become good stewards of what we have been given, then we can bless the rest of the world.

I agree that we have a responsibility to give because we have been given much, but charity begins at home and we should start with our people here that need help. We should be an example to the world first.

Social Security

Obviously, the system as it is will not continue to work. We have literally tens of thousands of senior citizens turning sixty-five every day, and this will continue until the year 2025. We have to fix the program. The problem with fixing the problem is this.

Right now, the money collected in social security from the workforce of America goes to pay the social security of the aged. As America ages, more and more senior citizens will begin to draw from the system and fewer and fewer working citizens will be contributing to the system. The money will run out. So how do we resolve the issue?

Two things have to happen. First, we have to find the money to fund the current population of recipients through to at least 2025. The best and only way that we can do this is to take that money from other areas and put it into the system. It will have to come out of the budget from wasteful spending, foreign aid, and other areas that should be cut. The good news is that there is enough money there to do it. (See the later section on the budget.)

The government would be able to subsidize this plan and not raise taxes. The biggest problem with making this happen is that our elected leaders are not going to loosen their greedy fingers from around this money without a fight. We have to take control of our money and make it work for our country and it's citizens-not for the politicians and their power.

The second thing that has to happen is that money collected from the working adults has to be invested for their retirement. For this, we have many options available, and each person would have the ability to choose their own plan just like they do now with their 401k programs. It is just a matter of setting up the program to draw the money out of their payroll and direct deposit it into their fund.

The added benefit of this plan would be that a ton of new money would influx into the stock market boosting our economy and our dollar. **What do ya know? A common sense answer that politicians will surely cry and cringe over**.

Of course, they will tell you that there is not enough money there to fix social security, but when you look at our national budget, you will find that when we start cutting off the fat, there is a lot of fat to cut off. I also have another way to pay for it so keep reading.

Welfare

Welfare should be a temporary fix only. Just like the plan on re-educating and retraining the unemployed, welfare should be a way to put the American back in the work force. We cannot continually give money to someone who is not a contributing member of society, if they do not plan to become one.

I spoke earlier of our responsibility to take care of our own. This is a two way street, and we as individuals must take responsibility for ourselves in becoming a productive member of society that contributes to the economy. That means if you don't work because you are lazy and sorry, then you better have some good friends or family to take care of you because the government handouts will have a cutoff date. The government will not pay you to sit in a subsidized apartment and watch soap operas. The government will not pay you to have babies without fathers. It does not matter if you are white, black, brown, yellow, or purple, the green will be to help you get back on your feet and get retraining and re-education, and it will have a time limit.

If you fail to take advantage of the opportunity given you to better yourself, you will suffer the consequences. The American taxpayer will not carry you indefinitely. You have to contribute to society and the economy.

We will discuss illegal immigration in a later chapter, but suffice it to say that, if you are an illegal immigrant from any country, under this program, you would receive absolutely no benefits of any kind in this country, unless the tax laws are changed which I propose later. You would be refused health care. Your women would not have hospitals allowing them to stay and give birth to your children. Not one tax dollar would be spent on any illegal immigrant in any way other than to round them up for detention or deportation. This sounds tough, I realize, but it must happen this way to allow for the money to fund the other projects that will benefit American citizens. Once again, the taxpayers in this country are not responsible for paying for others. We will help our own to help themselves for the betterment our society.

If the tax laws change as I propose them, then the immigrants would be eligible to receive the benefits of the healthcare system I have proposed because they will be paying into the tax base.

Health Care

Insurance Reform

This is a topic that has made many a national headline lately. Hillary is using this as a main point in her run for the Presidency, although her plan to actually make it happen doesn't hold water. You see, she doesn't plan to reduce wasteful spending and big government, so the truth is that she has no way of coming up with that much money to fund the program. She could not raise taxes enough to fund a national healthcare program and keep all the other fluff in the budget, so with her, it is an idle promise.

Too bad. If she were an honest, ethical person who actually cared about the American people, she would run on a balanced budget platform to cut ALL the fat out, and then she would be able to **realistically** propose healthcare without burdening the taxpayers in this country.

Democrats, don't feel bad. The republicans running in this primary have no intention of making any changes that will benefit the American healthcare system either.

Common sense tells all of us that healthcare is too expensive and that the only people who are coming out in this situation are the doctors, hospitals, pharmaceutical companies, insurance companies, and attorneys.

We might take a look at the hybrid plan that Italy has in place, where private insurance is available for those who can afford it and choose to pay for it. Then there are the state doctors and facilities for those who cannot afford the cost of the private insurance or who choose the public system to save their premiums.
This actually seems like the best solution to our problem, and will still give people the incentives to become healthcare professionals.

With a national healthcare program, fair regulation could occur where the citizens of this country only would get medical coverage with incentives for healthy habits and lifestyles. Those who maintain unhealthy eating habits(i.e.-obesity) and lifestyle choices(i.e.-smoking) would pay penalties for their healthcare. Public doctors, hospitals, and pharmaceutical companies would get a fair price for their services, *while ambulance chasing attorneys(John Edwards) could apply for re-education and retraining funds.*

Here comes the right with their yelling that government regulation and intervention will lead to "big brother."

I say if you have a real, legitimate plan that is beneficial to the American people and not to yourself and your own power base, then lay it out or shut up and get out of the race for the election. You are not part of the solution-you are the problem.

And before you Democrats get all smug and giggly, government regulation in one area to make it better for the people does not mean "carte blanche" to set up big tax and spend government in all areas. I only propose government regulation in two areas and this is one. In other words, we must use common sense to exercise restraint of power abuse. The democrats know nothing about exercising restraint when it comes to spending tax dollars. Neither do republicans.

When the real power is in the hands of the people, then we can make the right decisions through the right process to get the right result. The right process is to have three options on healthcare to give to the people to vote on.

Let the people choose.

Taxes

Here's a topic for the ages. *Can anyone say Boston Tea Party?*

Everyone hates paying taxes, and rightfully so. It is a pain to have to pay taxes. It is a pain to have to understand (or try to understand) our tax laws that change every year. It is a pain to keep up with what deductions we can take so we can keep as much of our money as possible that we worked so hard for. Most Americans have to take their taxes to an accountant or tax company to have their taxes done each year because it is just to complicated to do it yourself. This costs even more money and adds to the frustration level.

There is something we can do about it though. Several plans have been proposed that would completely eliminate all federal income taxes and abolish the IRS. The most recent one I heard about was the "fair tax." It basically proposes a twenty-three percent tax on all new goods purchased. The only problem with this is that it does not take into account funding additional programs like national health care. It also would cause millions of Americans to start buying all used items, which would create a drain on the economy.

There is a hybrid solution that works like the fair tax but would be absolutely fair and feasible to implement health care along with it and pay for it. It is a two-fold program that would eliminate all other federal taxes and state income taxes as well. I call it the "straight tax."

The straight tax is exactly that-an eighteen percent tax on every good sold for consumption except grocery and prescription medicines, and real estate(principle home) or automobiles(excluding luxury vehicles).

In other words, end user products would be subject to the tax. This means that products purchased for the manufacture of goods would not be taxed, thereby lowering costs of production, resulting in lower retail prices. This would help to cushion the tax across the board.

This would result in every person, **American or illegal immigrant**, paying their fair share of taxes, because every one purchases at their level of income. Let me give you a good example.

When Joe "big business man" goes out to buy that brand new Mercedes Benz SL65 to impress his next trophy ex-wife, he will pay eighteen percent of the $100,000 to $150,000 price in federal taxes. At a $100,000 price tag, that equals $18,000 in taxes(add to that the higher import taxes). When you (average citizen at $50,000 a year) go to buy your next "made in America" Toyota at $25,000, you will not pay any taxes. Everyone gets more in their check, because no one will pay any federal taxes including social security, FICA, state income tax, and no employers will pay payroll taxes or unemployment taxes.

No one will have any liability for capital gains taxes or estate taxes. No penalties for married couples. No rushing to beat an April 15th deadline. The IRS would be abolished except to keep a check on our politicians. Those employees could go to work for the FDA. **There would be no more evading taxes by anyone-not illegal immigrants, not rich people who can afford great accountants and attorneys, not politicians-no one!**

You may ask, "what about those living at or below the poverty level? Will they have to pay this tax also?" Those people living below the poverty level, if they are citizens, would be issued tax exemption cards that they will present each time they make a purchase. This card would exempt them from paying the full amount of the tax, and would only charge them eight percent.

To receive this card, they must be willing to submit to a retraining and re-education program where they would learn new job skills, and would receive assistance in job placement at the end of the training. At that point, their card would be voided, and they would pay the regular tax with each purchase. (This scenario supposes that they are not disabled in some way.)

The second tier of the tax program is not a tax in itself-it is voluntary. You ask **"who in the world would pay a voluntary tax?"** Those millions of people who play lotteries will. That's right. I propose a national lottery to help add to the income in the nation's budget. This will give us enough money to fund the programs necessary to the citizen's of this country, and to pay off the national debt, and provide for a strong military, and everything else that we need in this country.

Remember, I am not talking about socialism here. **I am talking about realistic ways to pay for the programs that we need**. I am not in favor of government giveaway(entitlement) programs except in the case of healthcare.

You won't hear any of the candidates for President in the upcoming elections give you any real ideas on how they are going to bring about change because they are not going to bring about any change. **They can't pay for change** without letting go of their power hold on America. They are not going to bring change because they are not willing to live off of what you and I have to live off of.

They don't care about how much is wrong with our current tax system because they still control all of the money and they are the beneficiaries.

They do not believe in giving the power to the people to vote on the major issues of our day, including our terrible tax system. In fact, I am convinced that with more money coming in to the system, the first thing our current politicians would do would be to vote themselves a huge pay raise with increased benefits and better pension than they have now. That is why they can no longer control the money.

I propose a new law that would make the budget a national agenda to be voted on by the American people.

It must be balanced. It must be concise and to the point. It must be completely free of special interest pork spending. I envision a lean, fiscally strong America in which the citizens of this great country can have a copy of the national budget in their hands and can read and understand it. You could go line by line and see where your tax dollars are going and exactly how they are being spent, and still make sense of it all.

With a national referendum on the budget, you the voter, can decide if the government is doing the right thing. This will guarantee that the federal government will not be involved in multi-million dollar parks in some state that you have never been to. It will guarantee that money will be allocated to each state equally for the individual states to decide what projects to fund and what not to.

I realize that this will require a total revamping of the current system that we have in place, but I, for one, feel it is time, and I know that there are millions more of American citizens who believe it is time for a change.

Together, we can!!!

Interest Rates

This is an area that most people are not very knowledgeable of and most choose not to think about. I agree. I personally believe the current system of the Fed regulating the interest rate is working quite well, and we should not try to fix something that is not broken.

I think we should set a cap on interest rates of ten percent, but we haven't been near twelve percent in quite a while, so this should not come into question anytime soon.

I do believe that we should set some limits or caps on interest rates that the sub prime market pays. We can be fair and establish rates that will be feasible for lenders to still make money, yet fair to borrowers also.

I propose a maximum of fifteen percent interest that can be charged for any one purchase, regardless of the amount. Of course, more competition will keep these rates regulated even lower to attract the business.

Simple. Common sense. Enough said.

Annual National Budget

Our annual national budget is a tremendous volume that is gargantuan in scale and in waste. There is no sense in the budget being this large and this complicated and this wasteful. No business on earth would survive if they operated on our budgets that we pass yearly.

A budget has to balance.

No if's, and 's, or but's. Government has the responsibility to balance the budget and I propose an amendment to make that mandatory. This is the first step.

The next step to getting the budget lean and trim and fiscally responsible is to pass a line item veto. This would give the President the authority to "cut the crap." That's right. Get rid of the pork. We have to eliminate all of the useless, wasteful spending. It has to go. Our tax dollars cannot be continually used to fund projects that are not national responsibilities.

Did you know that in our budget proposal for 2008, the President asked for a cap of $932 billion for "discretionary funds?" Of course, that was not enough for congress, so they used the "emergency funds" loophole to add another $21.3 billion to those "discretionary funds."

Those discretionary funds go to pay for the most idiotic things like a $4,511,978 program for off road recreational vehicles. Here's some more.

$6.4 million for a "wood utilization" research program

$1.3 million for berry research

$1 million paternity research for bears

$1 million for waterfree urinal conservation initiative

$500 thousand for a teapot museum

(Did you know that there was $25 billion that cannot be accounted for from 2003? That's right-no one knows where it went to-it just vanished)

And what about government contractors? They charge $20 for an ice tray, and the government pays it.

$5550 for a deep fryer that retails for $1950, and the government pays it.

Actually, you and I pay it with our tax dollars.

Look at NASA. Their 2008 budget is proposed at $17 billion 309 million 100 thousand. Have they found any men on Mars yet? Why are they interested in building a space station on the moon when we need to protect our ozone? When people here are hungry? When we need health care?

When we need to re-strengthen our military? Do we really need a probe to go out to the outermost reaches of the galaxy? And how do we know that the shuttle going through our ozone layer isn't causing part of the problem? I say privatize it if we must, but put our tax dollars to use in a productive way. By the way, if you get a chance, get on the internet and research how much equipment in dollars NASA cannot account for. It is in the billions.

How about the national endowment for the arts? Hey, I like art and think it is very important for our culture. I do not think that my federal tax dollars should go to fund starving artists. If anything, the individual states could make that decision with their share of funds.

Do you realize that with all of this money saved, we would be able to increase the rate of pay for our real heroes, the men and women who serve us in the military, police forces, and fire departments around this country?

OK. Enough of the examples of pork and entitlement programs. You get my point.

I also think that the budget(after the pork is eliminated) should be reviewed by leading economists for efficiency. A man with many advisors is seldom wrong. These advisors can help to whittle the budget down even more if need be, and help us get back to paying off the national debt. That would help the value of a dollar.

Once this has been done, then the budget as proposed can go out to the voters for their review. I am sure the media will be more than happy to assist in this endeavor. Then on national referendum day, the voters will get a chance to have their say and make their voice heard by ratifying the budget or by asking for more options. The only reason why the budget would be turned down would be if a majority of voters felt like more money should be put into other areas. Then those ideas could come out from the people and be looked at as a possibility for incorporation into the budget.

No, this part is not so simple, but **it is possible**, and it is right for the budget to be accessible to the American people. After all, it is your tax dollars, whether it be collected by the IRS or collected in sales tax. Don't you like the idea of knowing where your tax dollars are going?

The bottom line is this. Government does not have a license to take as much as they want and spend it as they deem appropriate. Right now, we have **TRILLIONS** of dollars in debt. That is absolutely unacceptable! It is not prudent. It is not wise. It cannot continue. That was not the intention of our founding fathers, and it is not the way it should be today or ever.

Foreign Policy

What should we do about foreign policy? Well, number one, we should realize that it is not our responsibility to take care of the rest of the world. Yes, we do have allies and interests that we should help to protect and/or foster, but I have already told you what I think about breaking the American bank to support other nations. We should do all that we can through diplomatic channels and the United Nations, without sending all our money overseas.

Next on the list, we should foster peace as much as we can from here. If the Arabs want to kill each other, let them. It is not our show. As far as I am concerned, we have an agreement with Israel and will fight with her to protect her right to exist and not give up any more land to any Arabs. They have the entire rest of the region, and can split it up any way they want. Who cares, but when they come to take on Israel, they take on the big, bad wolf too.

As far as this so called war on terror goes, President Bush needs to get a clue. Cut off the head of the snake and you will do extreme damage, even if someone else steps in to take his place. If we were really looking for Usama Bin Laden, and we know he is in the mountains of Pakistan, don't you think we would have found him by now? My strategy would be from the start, send 100,000 troops over there and find the sorry excuse for a human being and bring his head back-**with or without the body**!

What about Iraq? It is good that Saddam Hussein is gone. But what now? If you remember correctly, we supported him in the Iran-Iraq war and that is how he got the SCUD missiles. Everytime we help someone over there, it later comes back to haunt us. That's why I say no more getting involved in their matters. Of course, now we are already there and it is to late to say we were wrong. What do we do from here?

Win!!! Do not let this be another Vietnam. Crush the resistance. Build our base there. Put our government in place. That's what this is all about anyway. Just admit it and do it or get out. I say better yet, let the people vote on what they think we should do. Include it on a national referendum. **Power to the people**!

I do believe in having a super strong military and operating from a position of strength in every negotiation. I believe we should beef up our military and spend more dollars on that and less on trying to keep some governments in place and getingt others to fall.

The point I make is that we spend the money on our people and their salaries and their families. Not on the people of other nations. We can work through the United Nations on most issues when we need to, although I would reserve the right to part from the UN if it were in the best interest of American citizens.

Our foreign policy is simple. We will do what is best for America first and foremost. We will push our interests throughout the world, but we will spend our money to make our people better.

I would like to add one little tidbit here that I feel is important and is becoming more important to the election coming up. It has less to do with foreign policy, and more to do with interrogation of political prisoners. Waterboarding is now the buzz word issue in the Presidential debate. Almost every candidate has come out against waterboarding of prisoners.

Let's think about this for a moment and apply some common sense to the issue. Our people are under attack. New terror cells are discovered frequently within our own borders. Plans to attack our military bases are uncovered by the FBI, CIA, NSA, Homeland Security, DEA, or any other police agency. These prisoners have a connection with terrorists overseas who more than likely trained them, supplied them with intelligence, financed their operation, and gave them the go ahead to commit acts of terrorism on American soil.

Now, what I don't understand is why we aren't stringing them up by their gonads in public to get any information we can about their infrastructure, other cell members, other cells operating within our borders, and names and locations of contacts here and overseas. Not only would I recommend waterboarding, I would also recommend **wetting them down completely and applying electric shock therapy to them to get the answers we want**. I would support burning them with a lit cigarette(don't you love the old movies?) until they talk.

After we get their information and we are sure they have nothing else to tell us, they should be tried as traitors and we should cut their heads off, and videotape it for the internet so their leaders could see that we will not tolerate them in our country, period!!! **That is what they have done to our people, is it not?**

If you are a pansy liberal who thinks we should never torture anyone, then I suggest we let the prisoner come live with you, and you can be responsible for this violent criminal. I bet your spouse and kids may have a problem with that.

I know some of you may not like what I say, but hey, it's my book. If you don't like it, go write your own. Just don't be afraid to tell the truth as it really is-not the politically correct, watered down version. If they had killed your family member, I bet you would support it!

ENERGY

What is the first thing you think of when you read that word-energy? Oil, right? Well, that should not be. This shows just how dependent we have become on petroleum products here in the good old U.S. of A.

Before we get started here, let me just say that I am not an Al Gore fan and do not believe that our world is in as much danger as he proclaims that it is. I do, however, believe that we have been doing a great deal of harm to our environment. I also believe we have a responsibility to our world and we are to be good stewards while we are here for our future generations.

This is why I am amazed that that the U.S. pulled out of the Kyoto Protocol and decided that "we aren't ready for that here," according to Harlan Watson, state department senior climate negotiator and representative to the Bali conference.

Let me spell this out to you in plain English. George Bush cannot let go of his tight connections with the big oil companies and coal companies, so he won't commit to reducing emissions in this country at a rapid rate or on a short timetable. He also will not mandate to energy companies that they must hasten research and development so that we can untie ourselves from the chains of foreign oil dependency.

There are many options out there for us and many companies are doing all they can to speed up the process of R&D so they can bring a suitable product to market quickly, which will allow us to be cleaner, greener, and not dependent at all on foreign products. Google is one of these companies and I applaud their efforts. There are many more that are working to this end, and to them, we all owe a big thank you. There are new wind, steam, and solar projects, as well as various types of ethanol development going on right now.

There has to be more, though, and we have to do it faster than the current trends. If you listen to any newscasts at all, you have heard that our current leadership are hoping to have things changing by 2025 and before 2050. That's a load of bull. It is only because he owes big business that Bush won't commit to a faster plan like the majority of the other nations have. For example, the European union has committed to a twenty percent reduction of emissions by 2020, and that is really taking to long in my opinion.

The Kyoto protocol is looking for a twenty five to forty percent reduction by 2020. That is better, but still to long. If Exxon-Mobil had taken twenty billion of the thirty nine and a half billion in profit last year(2006) and added it to it's R&D department, we might have some very positive new ideas to look at very soon. Not so for the number one company on Forbes list of most profitable. Yes, they did have money budgeted for R&D, like all other companies, but they have not taken the lead as they should have. They have been the worst example of capitalistic greed this nation has ever seen, and the environment is not as important as another billion dollars to them.

We as individuals should also look for ways to be cleaner and greener for our environment. There are websites now on the internet that will teach you how to use localized solar power, wind power, and other sources of power to heat your home, water, and provide electricity. Hopefully very soon, the auto makers will have cars that run on completely alternative fuel sources. I have seen where Honda has come out with a new "fuel cell" vehicle that emits only water vapor-no harmful emissions whatsoever. Now that is progress.

We could solve most of our auto fuel problems right now by following the example of Brazil. They run all of their vehicles on fuel made from sugar. Sugar is plentiful. We could grow it in many of the states. Wouldn't that be a great way to help Louisiana get back on its feet after hurricane Katrina? What we couldn't grow, we could import from South America. From what I understand, this type of Ethanol burns cleanly, and would solve our auto emissions problem completely.

The problem is that the oil companies know this, our government leaders know this, but they won't do anything about it. It's all about the Benjamins.

You, however, can look for ways that you can have a positive impact on your environment because that is just what it is-yours. Your air to breathe, your water to drink, your earth to preserve. Don't you want a better earth for yourselves and your children?

If so, then it is finally time for you to get involved in making this world a better place. Ultimately, it is not the government's responsibility to make change, but ours. We have to begin the changes. We have to push our leaders to do the right thing. We have to convince them that they vote for a better future or we vote them out. Plain and simple!

If we had a national referendum day, we would have some very viable options to look at, and then we the people could vote for the best choice. That would take the big money lobbyists right out of the problem.

Armed Forces

We have closed bases. We have cut jobs. We have decreased the size and strength of our military. Why? To save money? Re-read the economy-budget section of this book. We are cutting costs in the wrong areas. Granted, I am sure the military pays to much for the products and services they purchase from contractors, and these costs should be analyzed and adjusted, if necessary, to fall into line with normal costs. We should not be cutting out our military strength though.

If we were to make the changes that I propose to the budget, there would be more than enough money to build our military in a lean, fiscally responsible fashion. We could increase jobs. We would not be closing bases.

I propose that all high school graduates who are physically and mentally fit be required to serve one year in the military immediately after graduation from high school. If we raise the pay rate for our servicemen and women, we would no doubt have many that would decide to stay in the military as a career. We also could continue to offer money to help pay for college after service, depending on the number of years served.

The bottom line is that we have to have a strong, prepared military to meet the needs of our country, and defend ourselves and our allies in this ever-controversial world. Our armed forces must be a priority.

Of course, you, the voter, would have the final say in this when you vote on it on national referendum day. It would be in your hands.

Keep in mind though, that whenever we have operated from a position of strength, we have had favorable results. Reagan was the best at this in my lifetime. He spoke loudly but carried an even bigger stick. He was able to get congress to work with him because he knew how to win, and not just fight endlessly. He believed in a strong military. He believed in building our defenses and weaponry. He knew that our enemies could not be trusted to keep treaties they had signed. He knew that diplomatic channels were good only for so long. He was not afraid to show force and muscle, and when he did, the world took notice.

Today, we wage a new kind of war. This war on terror is an ongoing war with factions of many nations in the middle east, Europe, South America, and even right here in our homeland. We have to start thinking differently about how to defend ourselves and our country. We have to educate ourselves and our families about our enemies, and be vigilant and watchful. We have to prepare ourselves to fight should the need ever arise. We have to be ready to face the ugly truth of this new war-**that it could be on our doorstep tomorrow morning.**

Our freedoms that we so often take for granted are at risk. Our children's future will depend on how we respond to the call of freedom today.

Crime and Punishment

Here is a topic that will alienate a lot of you. Crime is ridiculous in this country. There is no value placed on a human life or on personal property. Again, greed is a large contributing factor to a majority of the crimes. Race is a factor in many crimes. A new and emerging factor is anger, depression, and what we would call being "unbalanced." This is the case in many of the multiple shootings recently.

The bad thing about it is that I can remember a time when I was growing up just a few short years ago(30) when we didn't lock the doors at night. We did live in the country at the time, but it was more the attitude than the location. We did not live in fear. That has changed drastically. I rarely even go to the mall anymore because of the gangs and thugs hanging out on the inside, and the carjackers outside. Come on now. If these are your kids, you should be going to jail with them as far as I am concerned because you are just as responsible. Of course, you won't accept responsibility. It's society's fault, right? TV raised your kids and taught them their values. **Like I said, there should be a cell for you too.**

Anyway, what do we do about it now that it is out of hand?
Our prisons are over full, yet crime is getting worse and worse.

Well, if you ask any liberal, they will tell you that we have to start when kids are young. We have to lift their self-esteem and not scold them or reprimand them. We can't tell them they are not making the grade-they can't be left behind. Don't take a chance on hurting their feelings. Make sure you treat them with political correctness. No spanking. No discipline.

Of course, part of this is correct. We should start when they are young and try to lift their self-esteem when they do something right and good. We should not, however, let them think that they are perfect and above discipline. There are both positive and negative consequences for our choices all throughout life and children have to be taught this early. They have to understand that when they make the wrong decisions, there will be a consequence. When they make a right decision, there will be a reward. Then, we have to teach them right from wrong, and contrary to the belief of some, **this is not subjective**.

This starts early in the home. It is the parents' responsibility. It is not the school system's responsibility to teach your child right from wrong, manners, courtesy, respect, and obedience. If you think it is, then there is a good chance you will be visiting your child on Sundays at the penitentiary.

What example as a country do we set to change the tide of crime? Number one is that the penalty has to be as severe as the crime itself. This is not cruel and unusual punishment. **This is fair and equitable punishment.** It is what the criminal deserves.

Remember, it's called PUNISHMENT!!!

It's not supposed to be working out, lying around watching tv, playing basketball, etc. Again, it's called punishment. It is happening because the person in question committed a **CRIME**!!!

I know these are really big words for liberals, but try to work through it if you can. Education is a good way to help the rehabilitation process, but the best way to ensure that a convict doesn't end up back in jail is to make the punishment severe enough that they never, ever want to do anything that might make them return to this place. In other words, **hard labor, hard conditions, very restricted visitations, no luxuries whatsoever**. Prison is not the rec center.

I propose prisons in the desert also. Set up a perimeter fence, a few guards, one building with beds and mess hall, and drop food supplies in weekly. The prisoners would all get up at six am and work until sundown daily. What kind of work, you ask? Dig a hole here two feet deep by two feet wide. When you finish that hole, fill it back up by digging another just like it over here. Then another and another. That's right. Good, honest, hard work. In fact, forget the fence. If they want to run away in the middle of the desert, let them. That's one less mouth for the taxpayers to feed. That will make someone think very hard about what they did and what they want to do from now on. It also would save the taxpayers a lot of money.

Of course, this is for crimes of a lesser nature. I also am an advocate of cutting off someone's finger if they are caught stealing. Maybe it is a little rough, but I would be willing to bet they will do everything they can before they steal again.

What about more serious crimes? Easy. Pick a crime.

How about child molesters? Are you kidding me? Someone hurts a defenseless child. First offense-castration. Second offense-a nationally televised execution. WHAT? No way you say. Well, I thought you said you wanted to be tough on crime. I thought you said you wanted it to stop. Yeah, but… But nothing.

The way we have been doing it for the last thirty years is only increasing crime rates because there is no real punishment-no consequence! The biggest breeding ground for crime is in prison. Criminals develop networks of people and resources in prison.

They make plans for their departure as if they were arrested only to get a bigger score. Forget it! **Punish the criminals correctly and you will have fewer criminals.**

Murder? If convicted, a nationally televised execution. And I am not talking thirty years after the crime was committed. No laying up on the taxpayers dollar forever. Two appeals-that's it. Maximum of two years from the date of original conviction. If the verdict is not overturned, you become an example for the youth of America to **not** do what you have done. If you have taken a life, you deserve to have yours taken, and it the government's job to do this.

Of course, self-defense cases are exceptions. The reason. You try to carjack me, rob me, assault me, and I will be sending you to meet your maker. The court will not have to worry about what to do with you. And hopefully, there are more and more Americans out there arming themselves to defend against the perpetrators of these crimes.

I haven't forgotten about all those white collar criminals either. That's right. **No more country club federal pen for you**. It's right in the middle with the general population. If you survive, you certainly will not commit a crime again.

Whatever the crime, a hard line approach is what we have to have to make a difference in our society. We cannot continue to think that a slap on the hand and a "play nice" is going to change someone's behavior patterns.

Now if we can just get our judges to get their heads screwed on straight, and put the criminals behind bars instead of the innocents, we may be ok. So let's talk about that for a moment.

Explain to me how someone who is known to have committed a crime-we are talking witnesses galore, forensic evidence, the works-can get off on a technicality. For example, the case of Mr. Nichols, who just happened to shoot up an Atlanta courtroom, in full view of everyone in the court. He is saying that he did not get appropriate legal representation because of the indigent defense fund being inadequate, and his attorneys petitioned the court for more money to represent him. **Give me a freaking break**.

This guy doesn't deserve any more or better defense at all. This guy deserves to be strung up in the courtyard of the courthouse in full view of the public for what he did. There is no shortage of witnesses. There is no lack of forensic evidence. They have the gun. The bullets match. People are dead, and this guy is getting break after break. Will someone just put this guy out of our misery, please?!!

And there are so many more cases like this. Of course, everyone is entitled to due process under the law, but how stupid do we have to be with it? If the judges in this country would do the right thing for the victims and the rest of the citizens instead of worrying about the criminal's rights, we would have far fewer criminals running around making our society unsafe for the law abiding citizens.

Again, I encourage every-law abiding citizen to carry a weapon to defend yourself. Learn how to use it properly. Practice with it continually at the firing range. Become proficient with it. It may save your life one day or the life of someone very close to you. And hopefully, you will be a good enough shot that the court system will not be burdened with another criminal.

Another change that will make a large difference in crime is the salary that we pay our officers to put their lives on the line everyday. With the changes that I propose to the budget, cities and states would have enough money to pay more to law enforcement officers, and be able to pay more of them. We certainly could use more police on the streets to make our neighborhoods safer.

The biggest key to making a difference in our judicial system would be that no judges would be appointed. They would all be elected by the people. They would be accountable to the people.

The bottom line is that whether you are for or against capital punishment, you would have your opportunity to vote your belief in a national referendum for the people. This would be one of the biggest issues on any ballot, and the people should have their say, either for or against. Let the people make the final decision. Power to the people! Hey, if you think I am crazy, vote!

Gun Control

Well, after reading the last chapter(you did read it, didn't you?), there will not be a big surprise in this chapter.

If we outlaw guns, then only the outlaws will have guns.

It's true. Think about it for a moment. We pass a law to ban all guns. OK. Every law abiding citizen will now refrain from any attempt to purchase a firearm because…well, it's illegal, and they are law abiding citizens.

But what about the criminals? Do you think if we pass a law outlawing guns that the criminals are going to respect that law and not go looking for weapons to purchase? Get a clue, Mr. or Ms. ignorant! In fact, now that we have taken away the right for citizens to own guns to protect themselves, we will have made them completely and utterly vulnerable to the criminals **who will get guns**. This also will create a tremendous black market for guns in which the criminals tend to operate anyway. So here we are, you and I, law abiding citizens with no guns, and the criminals know that. What chance do we have? Look at Washington D.C. as the perfect example. Look at New York.

So now you think I am a card-carrying member of the NRA. Not so. In fact, I believe there are some things that should not be. No one should have automatic weapons. If semi-automatic is not good enough for you, then you must have bad intentions or you plan to defend yourself against a SWAT team. Pistols for home protection and for carrying in the car are great. Make sure you understand and are practiced in the art of using it.

I understand the NRA position of limiting any government intrusion into the right to bear arms and I agree with that completely, but can't we agree to meet in the middle and use some common sense about the issue? I don't want the government telling me I can't have a gun for my own protection either, but I don't necessarily have to have an automatic assault rifle.

So much for my opinion on the matter. The most important opinion on the matter is yours, the voter's. Gun control should be on a national referendum where you as a registered voter would be able to voice your opinion on this issue. Again, the power of the people is in the vote. **For the people, By the people!**

Abortion

OK. All joking from the first section aside. This is a serious issue that needs to be given the proper respect that it deserves. The reason is that this is a moral issue that most Americans feel very passionately about in one way or the other. Whether you are pro-choice or pro-life, most Americans have a solid opinion about the topic. I was too young to be following politics and the Supreme Court when Roe v. Wade hit the spotlight. I wish I had been older and attentive to the issues at hand so that I may more thoroughly understand all the viewpoints and arguments presented.

I admit that I am pro-life because of my Christian upbringing, yet pro-choice because I dislike government intervention. Common sense dictates that the debate should begin at the beginning. What I mean is "where does life actually begin?" and "when does abortion become murder of a human life, if ever?"

My personal opinion(and many doctors back up this opinion) is that life begins when the baby's(fetus's) heartbeat can be detected. If there is a heartbeat, there is a life. Therefore, I have to base my opinion on abortion on this pre-supposed belief. Whenever the baby(fetus) has a heartbeat that can be detected, that is a child, and as such, has every right to life as any other human being born on

American soil. Neither the mother nor the father has the right at that point to deny life to a living creature.

The reason I believe that this is a perfect point for distinction is that there is a physical measurement to guide us. This is a measurable, physical attribute that cannot be disputed. When there is a heartbeat, there is a life.

There are arguments that the fetus(baby) is not a living being if it cannot sustain life outside the womb. Some would even go so far as to say that the fetus should not be considered a life until it is delivered. These people would be in favor of third trimester abortions.

I am not a woman so I cannot imagine the emotions of discovering an unwanted pregnancy. I am alive, however, and I can imagine the possibility that my mother could have chosen to destroy me before I was born. This doesn't set well with me. What about you? What if your mother had chosen to abort you? What if you were just an inconvenience? What if you didn't matter enough to your mother to even be given a chance at this life? Kinda makes you think, huh?

Therefore, I believe the position should be agreed upon that once a heartbeat is detected, abortion would be murder.

Now, this position along with a few other possibilities, would go to the voters in a referendum, so they would and should have the opportunity to vote their moral conscience, and put American policy in place. Whether you agree with my beliefs or not, you should have the right to have a say in the making of our national policy concerning this matter. Our Supreme Court and Legislators should not be making this decision for us. Our three parties should come up with three options for the American people, and the people should vote their beliefs.

Definition of Marriage

This is another moral issue that has recently come to the forefront of the national spotlight. The biggest proponents of a change to the current definition of marriage are gays that want to be able to wed a person of the same sex. I could see where some folks who believe in multiple partners might benefit from this type of legislation also.

Although national debate has made this an area of concern, I don't believe that the majority of the American people would vote for a change in the current definition of marriage. Again, the minority are attempting to force their will on the majority.

I believe most Americans feel as I do on this issue. That opinion is this. If you want to be gay, by all means, go and be as gay as you want to be in your own home, but quit flaunting it all over to get yourself noticed, and trying to get others to accept you when they don't have to. We straight people do have a choice, ya know. If you can accept yourself being gay, then that should be all you need. You do not need approval from the rest of America, and quite frankly, you are probably not going to get it.

If you want changes to laws, then you should be willing to let the entire population of America vote on those changes, and if you get the votes, the laws will be changed. If not, work for next time.

That is the great thing about a national referendum. Every idea has an equal opportunity. It is a level playing field. If you are successful, maybe I will go out and get seven wives so I can celebrate your victory with you. You never know. (I wonder how many pairs of shoes seven wives would have?)

Immigration Reform

OK, here is a topic that has been at the forefront of public debate quite a bit lately. We have had everything from the Governor of New York trying to give drivers licenses to illegal immigrants to Oklahoma passing tough laws against the illegals causing them to flee in droves and hurt the housing market because contractors can't find workers(at least not for what they were paying the illegals.)

Let's start with the basics if we are going to apply common sense to this issue. The basics are these-these people are immigrants who are here in this country illegally. That's right. They are breaking the law by being here in this country. From that point of view is where we must begin to operate.
Now, what are the pros and cons of the illegal immigrants being in this country? Let's start with the pros to give them a fair shake.

Most illegal immigrants here are Mexicans. The majority of the whole debate is about Mexicans. As such, let's skip the politically correct crap and we will call them Mexicans for the sake of discussion.

The Mexicans work harder and longer than most Americans are willing to. They have a much stronger work ethic when it comes to manual labor type positions. These positions used to be filled by the less educated whites and blacks, but now employers can get Mexicans to do more work in less time for less money. It doesn't take a genius to figure out that this equates to more profit for the employer. It normally results in better quality work for the customer also. These people are doing the work that no one else wants to do nowadays. For this, I must give them their credit that is due. They work on farms. They work in construction. They work in landscaping. They work on roads. They do the hard work. Bravo.

Now, let's look at the cons of them being in this country. Our hospitals refuse no one health care if they need it. Who pays for it? American taxpayers-that's who! In Dallas, Texas, there is a hospital that has hired translators because over fifty percent of births are now to illegal immigrants who do not speak English. Who is paying for their services? American taxpayers. California is giving away the world because of all the illegal immigrants there. It is totally out of control, and the problem is worsening. Many are working illegally, but there are many others also who are stealing social security numbers to be able to work within the system.

And what about crime? The crime rate among illegal immigrants is the fastest rising rate in the country.

So what are the common sense solutions to our problem here. Well, it would be really hard to round them all up and send them all back, and it would cost the taxpayers a ton of money. We also cannot let them continue to live here under the radar and not pay for the services they are getting.

Simple!!! With my proposed tax plan-the straight tax-they will pay their fair share in taxes just like everyone else and then be entitled to the services they receive like education and healthcare.

Think about it. Instantly, the tax base would be increased by ten to twenty million!!!

They would be required to obtain a social security number to receive any services in healthcare or to have their kids attend a public school. Of course, it would be automatically mandatory that, should they decide to stay in our great country, they would have to learn the language-period! We should never be buying textbooks from Mexico so we can teach in Spanish here in this country. **This is not the United States of Mexico.** It is America and we speak English. Learn it or leave it. This would be included in the test for naturalization for citizenship that also would be mandatory. They would have to take an oath of allegiance to America. They would have to learn the Pledge of Allegiance. They would have to learn "God Bless America." In ENGLISH!!!

Next, the border would be closed and their relatives would have to come in the right way.

Also, any immigrants that commit crimes against Americans would lose their citizenship and be deported immediately. We have no place in this country for criminals-Mexican, white, black, or other. (We've already talked about crime in detail in another chapter.)

Now, let me say that I have known several Mexicans. The ones I knew personally were here legally. There were many that I met who were here illegally. They worked on the peach farms in the area, and were very hard workers. They paid their bills-in cash. They were never any trouble in the area. If they had spoken good English, they would have been a-ok with me-as long as they were paying taxes.

I have been to Mexico back in 1984. You want to talk about a poverty stricken country that will make you cry for the people there. Mexico is it. I can't blame the people for wanting to come to our country. I would if I were living there. They can be very poor in this country and still be better off than they are there. I have compassion on them. I also know that they have to pay their fair share of our costs and obey our laws.

I believe the majority of Americans feel the same way I do. I don't think we should just open the borders and let them all come in. In fact, we have to slow our growth in order to firm up our infrastructure to meet the demands of the growth. We have to catch up. The point is that we can if we do it the right way, and we will have the money to pay for it when the illegal immigrants are paying taxes.

Illegals Costing US Taxpayers More Than Iraq War

$11 Billion to $22 billion is spent on welfare to illegal aliens each year.

$2.2 Billion dollars a year is spent on food assistance programs such as food stamps, WIC, and free school lunches for illegal aliens.

$2.5 Billion dollars a year is spent on Medicaid for illegal aliens.

$12 Billion dollars a year is spent on primary and secondary school education for children here illegally and they cannot speak a word of English

$17 Billion dollars a year is spent for education for the American-born children of illegal aliens, known as anchor babies.

$3 Million Dollars a DAY is spent to incarcerate illegal aliens.

30% percent of all Federal Prison inmates are illegal aliens.

$90 Billion Dollars a year is spent on illegal aliens for Welfare and Social Services by the American taxpayers.

$200 Billion Dollars a year in suppressed American wages are caused by the illegal aliens.

The illegal aliens in the United States have a crime rate that's two-and-a-half times that of white non-illegal aliens. In particular, their children, are going to make a huge additional crime problem in the US.

During the year of 2005 there were 4 to 10 MILLION illegal aliens that crossed our Southern Border also, as many as 19,500 illegal aliens from Terrorist Countries. Millions of pounds of drugs, cocaine, meth, heroin and marijuana, crossed into the U.S from the Southern border. Homeland Security Report.

The National Policy Institute, "estimated that the total cost of **mass deportation would be between $206 and $230 billion or an average cost of between $41 and $46 billion annually over a five year period.**"

In 2006 illegal aliens sent home $45 BILLION in remittances back to their countries of origin.

Nearly One Million Sex Crimes Committed by Illegal Immigrants In The United States.

Total cost is a whopping $338.3 BILLION A YEAR!!!

Race Relations

We must start out with a premise to discuss this topic. If you are serious and honest about wanting to improve race relations in this country through dialogue, then you will read this section in its' entirety. This is dialogue.

I sincerely doubt that there are any white people living today in 2008 that were slave owners. I also doubt sincerely that there are any black people alive today in 2008 that were slaves. That is our premise.

Based on that premise, we can go forward. Public schools have been integrated for forty years. Blacks have had the same education as whites for forty years. Blacks have had affirmative action helping them to catch up in the workplace for forty years.

The politically correct crowd would have the whites believing that racism is a white institution and all whites are guilty of it, while people of color are immune. Many people have been stupid enough to accept this. It is even taught on some of our college campuses. This is ludicrous.

The truth is this, plain and simple. There are white people out there that do not like blacks simply because they are black. There are black people out there who do not like whites simply because they are white. It is a fact. It is not going to change because we try to make it change. Is it wrong? Of course, but you cannot tell someone how to feel. You cannot mandate that a certain person accept you-whether you be white, black, brown, gay, straight, muslim, jewish, or whatever else you want to throw in there.

There is another fact that cannot be ignored. It is not the majority of people who think this way. Most people in 2008 have grown up in a multi-cultural society, and think nothing of living alongside people of other races. It is a fact that the majority has accepted without question. Sadly, a small minority of people take sides on the issue, and keep it at the forefront of political debate as a heated topic.

The only way that race relations are going to improve in this country will be when each group agrees to be honest and take responsibility for the actions of their own group. There are improvements to be made on both sides, and individuals are the key to changes.

Until the leaders of the respective communities stop blaming the other race for their own problems within their communities, there will be no chance for real and lasting racial harmony. The victim mentality has to be dropped and aggression and discrimination must be made a thing of the past before success can be achieved. We have to be willing to give a leg up to anyone when we can. It is our duty and responsibility as fellow Americans.

Once this happens, real leaders can effectively work together to provide education that will be useful for the betterment of the individuals, and will help them to climb ladders of success, that will, in turn, be an inspiration to others that will follow. When this happens, then we can truly select the best person for the job without fear of discrimination or fear of the cry of discrimination.

We will be able to dismantle affirmative action policies that have been in place for long enough. We will be able to raise the standards of education for the betterment of all people and our society. We will become more productive as a society working together knowing that our co-worker deserves to be there because they are the most qualified. We will be able to trust the people in the system instead of saying the system is an entity on it's own with it's own agenda. We will be more competitive in the global marketplace, affording more opportunities for all people.

Then we can vote together for the best for our country and our fellow man, regardless of his or her color, free of entitlements and special interests, free of personal agendas, voting for the common good for all Americans.

This is the power of the people, for the people, by the people!

Political Correctness

This book would not be complete, in my opinion, without some comments on the evolution of political correctness and the speech police. We have seen the rise of media personnel, politicians, minorities, and any other group who could possibly be offended, lashing out at those who say things that they don't like.

Now let me start off by saying that I was brought up to believe that if you could not say something good, don't say anything at all. It seemed to work really well for kids, because of how hurtful kids can be sometimes. They don't start out knowing any better. They just say what comes to mind in reaction to what they experience. In other words, they simply are responding to their truth. It can be hurtful to others, though, so we teach our kids to curb their tongues.

What we are really teaching our kids, when we stop and think about it, is to **not** tell the truth. You see, I have done some careful observation on this. I have found that even when someone speaks the truth, if a certain group does not happen to like what is said, they condemn it and it makes the news, and the speaker is labeled as heretic, racist, cheauvanist, or whatever other label applies.

Political correctness then, has given us the mandate to not speak the truth, and has also given us license to not have to face the truth and deal with it. We can just brush it away and say that it is not reality. Again, the messenger gets shot.

Well, the truth of the matter is that many times, the truth hurts, and if someone is speaking the truth, then perhaps we should face the truth and try to find answers, rather than trying to hide the facts behind a veil of denial. The politicians do this every day, lashing out at the other party in the blame game. Some civil rights leaders do this to make excuses and shift blame. Hispanic leaders in this country are really getting into this trying to get the illegal immigrants accepted into this country with amnesty.

The whole issue is created by fear. We have become a nation, that in a large part, has become fearful of stating the obvious truth, because we are afraid someone will be offended. We are afraid of how people might label us if we are caught telling the truth.

Up until recently, these same groups that were constantly being offended by the truth, were not held to the same standard. They could say whatever they wanted, and it was not considered offensive. At least we have come to the point that the majority of us are being held to the same standard nowadays.

I want to close this chapter with a statement that comes straight from the Bible and has been used by

Americans throughout our entire history. "You shall know the truth, and the truth shall make you free." Pull no punches. Tell the truth even when it hurts. When the truth is out there, then we can deal with it.

Conclusion

Well, I hope that you found this book interesting, imaginative, and thought provoking. If I have caused you to question the current form of our government, then I have succeeded in my purpose. If I have caused you to question some of the issues addressed, then I have succeeded.

You do not have to agree with me on any of the issues. You do not have to agree with me on any of the proposals I have thrown out there as solutions to problems.

I am sure that you do agree with me, at least, that we have some issues within our governmental system that should be addressed and revamped or overhauled.

We are the greatest country in the world because of brave men who, over two hundred years ago, came together and set aside differences to create a government like no other the world had ever seen.

I hope that two hundred years from now, a greater, stronger America will look back and see brave men and women, who stood up and came together to form a new evolved and better system of government, still greater than any other the world has ever seen. I hope they will look back to you and to me.

Power To the People, For the People, By the People!!!

www.ingramcontent.com/pod-product-compliance
Lightning Source LLC
Chambersburg PA
CBHW022008170526
45157CB00003B/1199